The
Fox's Kettle

The Fox's Kettle

Story by Laura Langston

Illustrations by Victor Bosson

ORCA BOOK PUBLISHERS

AT the edge of the rice fields in old Japan lived a girl of rare and gentle beauty. Her name was Akoya and she was a gifted storyteller. Akoya lived with her parents in a small roadside inn. The inn was a peaceful, welcoming place where weary travelers could snack on rice balls and listen to Akoya spin her tales.

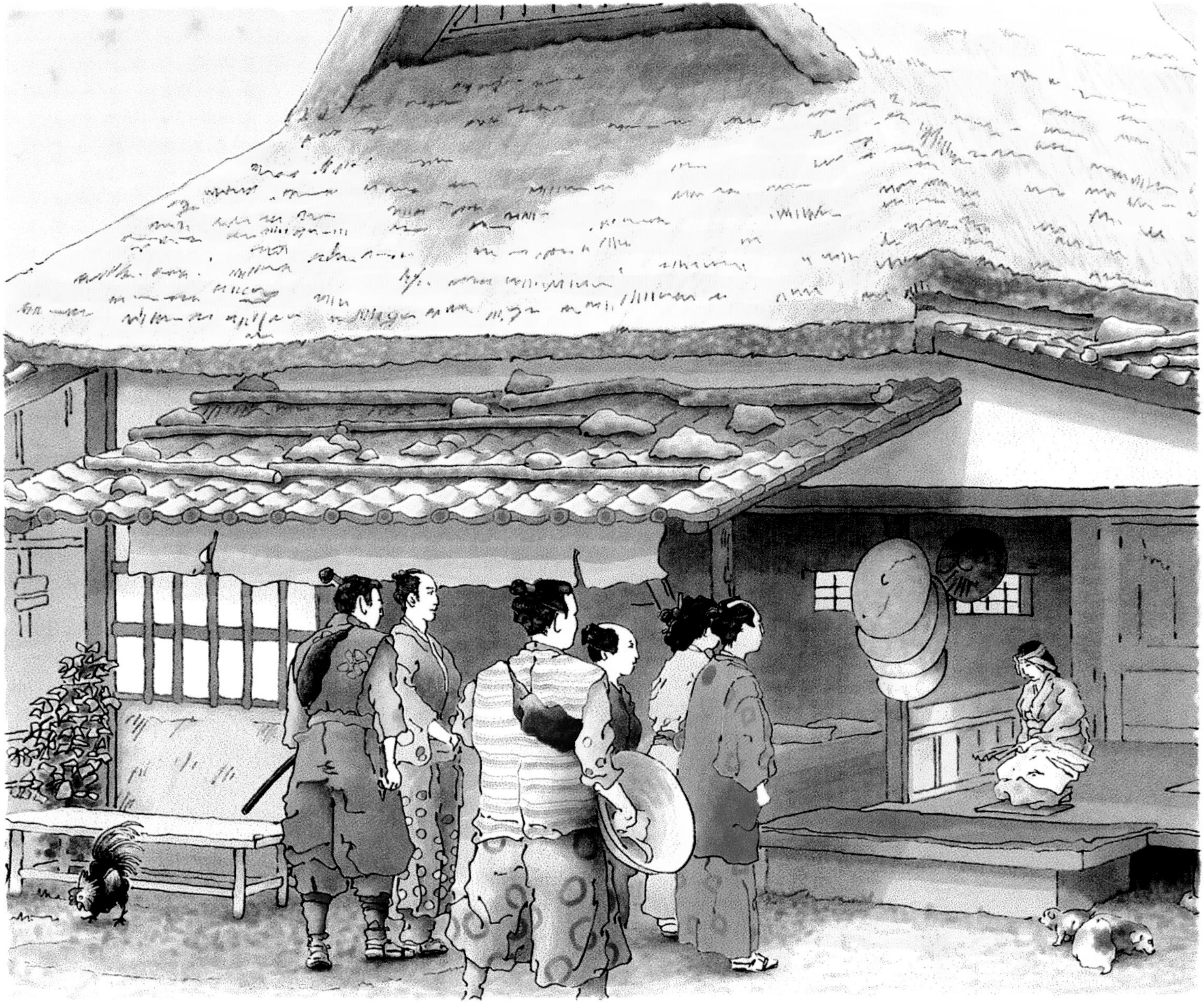

ONE night, when the moon hung in the sky like a great white ball of rice, a samurai appeared at the inn. "I am terribly hungry," the samurai said as he came inside. "I need food and drink."

"It is not a samurai, it is a fox," Akoya's parents whispered when they saw the creature's great, long nose. "Do not feed it."

Several travelers frowned. "You cannot trust a fox." They gulped the last of their meals and hurried out the door.

What the travelers said was true. Foxes were magical creatures who protected the rice harvest, but they could be kind or evil, depending on their nature.

"There is goodness in all creatures," said Akoya, who was brave as well as beautiful. "And no one should be allowed to go hungry. Whether he is fox or samurai, I will feed him." And as soon as her parents left the room, that is exactly what she did.

After he had eaten, the fox said, "I have no money to pay you. All I have is a big, black kettle. Since you have been kind to me, you may take it. When it is time to plant the rice and when the rice is ready to harvest, polish this kettle. If you care for it like your own child, rice will always grow in the village fields."

HEN planting time came, Akoya polished the kettle. To her surprise, out jumped three foxes. They ran in circles like happy dogs before they sat back on their hind legs and blinked their slanting eyes at Akoya. "Feed us well," they said, "and we will help you with the rice planting."

Akoya fed the foxes. When their bellies were full, the little creatures walked through the door leading to the fields. As they walked, they did what foxes do best. They turned into human beings. Akoya was overjoyed to see three strong men working her father's field. When all the rice was planted, the men returned to the inn. And this time, as they walked through the doorway, they turned back into foxes. Once again they ran in circles like happy dogs before sitting back on their hind legs and blinking their slanting eyes at Akoya.

"Quench our thirst," they said, "and we will protect all the rice in the village until it is ready to harvest."

Quickly Akoya gave them water. After drinking their fill, the foxes jumped back into the kettle, where they stayed silent and watchful until harvest time.

For several years all was well. The foxes protected the rice, Akoya cared for the foxes and the village prospered.

THEN the local landowner heard of the storyteller named Akoya. He sent a messenger to inquire about the young woman. When he learned she was more beautiful than cherry blossoms in spring time and her tales more magical than the nightingale's song, the landowner announced that Akoya would move to his mansion and become his official storyteller.

Akoya was saddened. Refusing the request of the landowner was not possible. He was the most powerful man in all the land. She simply had to go. When it came time to move, Akoya was forced to leave her few belongings — even the fox's big, black kettle — behind.

*S*OON it was planting time again and Akoya had to polish the kettle. She requested permission to go home for a visit. Reluctantly the landowner agreed. The inn was as peaceful and welcoming as Akoya remembered. Her parents were overjoyed to see their only child.

After greetings were exchanged, Akoya went to look for the big, black kettle. It was gone.

Her mother lowered her eyes. "Several months ago," she said, "an elegant samurai came looking for rice balls. I was about to feed him when I realized he was a fox. Quickly I chased him away. The next day, when I went to make tea, the kettle was gone."

FEAR pierced Akoya's heart. She had not watched the kettle like her own child. Nor had she been there to care for the foxes. She doubted if they would protect the harvest that year.

The foxes did not protect the rice. Every year for the next three years, the rice grew, but it was never harvested. First there was disease, then bad weather, then hungry animals ate it all up. People were forced to live on millet and barley. When those meager crops ran out, the people began to starve.

Finally the landowner made an announcement. "It is the fault of the foxes," he said. "They should protect our rice. Instead the villagers are starving. The foxes must be killed. Only then will rice grow tall and strong again."

BRAVELY Akoya stole away at midnight — the hour of the foxes. She traveled many miles through the night to find her fox friends. At last flashing eyes peered out of the darkness. One creature stepped forward, and Akoya recognized the samurai fox who had given her the kettle so many seasons before.

"You have not cared for the kettle like your own child, my lady." Akoya hung her head as the fox continued. "Since you left the inn, no one has fed us. No one cares for us, so we will not care for the rice crops."

"Then the villagers will starve," Akoya cried. "And the landowner says he will kill you all."

"He cannot kill us," the fox laughed. "We are magical, cunning creatures."

Akoya watched the foxes dance and play. One carried the big, black kettle in her arms. "Let me take the kettle to the landowner's mansion," Akoya begged. "I will feed you out the window at night when no one is watching."

The samurai fox shook his head. "The landowner will not allow the kettle in his house. And we will not eat food thrown out a window."

"The landowner's mansion?" asked a female fox who pranced back and forth in a rich purple gown. "It must be very beautiful there."

AKOYA could see envy flashing in those slanting fox eyes. "It is beautiful," she said. "Very, very beautiful." She told the female fox of luscious silks and delicate foods, of great paintings and wonderful banquets. She spoke of wealthy travelers from exotic lands who came bearing gifts.

"I would like that." The female fox flashed long, painted claws before Akoya. "I would like that very much."

"Perhaps you should change shape and take my place there," Akoya suggested.

The other foxes howled with laughter. "Though she is a great trickster, she could never fool the landowner," they said. "And if he discovers a fox has taken your place, surely he shall put you to death."

Akoya ignored the fear rising within. "I am willing to take that chance," she said courageously, "in order to return to the quiet life I once knew at the inn and to save the villagers from starving."

Silently the samurai fox considered Akoya's request. Finally he smiled. "You are a brave woman. Braver than the bravest samurai in all of Japan. Very well. We shall try."

So it was that the female fox did what foxes do best. She turned herself from fox to woman right before Akoya's eyes. Akoya sent her double in the direction of the landowner's mansion while she hurried home.

Word soon got back to the landowner that the storyteller Akoya had returned to the inn. "It cannot be," he bellowed angrily. "She lives here with me and is more beautiful than ever."

Akoya was summoned to him. Before leaving, she pulled on her oldest robe. She tangled her hair with knots, blackened her teeth with charcoal from the brazier and touched her cheeks with dust from the field.

KNEELING in front of the landowner, Akoya could see her fox double looking well fed and content. The landowner, meanwhile, looked stern.

"How can there be two women who look the same?" he demanded.

Akoya began her tale. "I have returned to my twin sister's side after being separated at birth."

The landowner raised an eyebrow. "Your sister?"

"Yes. Since my sister was more beautiful than I, my parents sent me to stay by the sea. They did not want me to wither away by growing in her shadow. But now that she lives in the splendor of your mansion, our shadows need never cross. And my lonely parents will have my company forever."

The landowner frowned. "There is no room in this village for two women who look so much alike. Tomorrow you return to the sea where you grew up."

Akoya bowed before the landowner. "Your excellency, I became a great tiller of the fields living by the sea. I know much about rice. Allow me two nights with my parents and I will make rice grow green and strong in your fields."

CREAT gasps filled the beautiful hall. The landowner stared at Akoya. "In two nights?" he asked.

"In two nights," Akoya promised.

Late that night, when the moon hung in the sky like a great ball of rice, Akoya polished the kettle. Out jumped the same three foxes who had protected the rice so many seasons before. Quickly Akoya explained the problem. Before too long, the inn was surrounded by foxes. Even though rice was usually planted in the cool light of morning, this time the foxes worked in the dark of night. And this time they didn't just plant the field surrounding the inn. They planted all the fields in the village.

The next day, the landowner sent for Akoya. "Very impressive for one woman to plant all the fields so quickly," he admitted. "But it is too soon in the year to plant rice. It is sure to wither and die with the frost tonight."

Akoya shook her head. "I think not," she replied.

OF course the rice did not wither and die with the frost at all. Once again, when darkness came, the foxes appeared at the inn. Because Akoya had fed them well all those years before, they were determined to help her now. They scattered through the rice fields and kept the young shoots warm and sheltered from frost the entire night.

THE next morning, Akoya was summoned to the landowner. He stood tall and proud in his fox-hunting clothes. "The rice grew three inches overnight," he said incredulously. "If this continues, no one will go hungry again." Akoya bowed low and hid her smile.

"You must not return to the sea," the landowner proclaimed. "You must stay in this village and teach us all you know about rice. And you must take this as a reward." Akoya was handed a silken purse filled with many gold pieces.

"No." Akoya folded her hands humbly in front of her. "Riches cannot make my heart brim over with happiness. Riches cannot make the rice in these fields grow green and strong."

The landowner frowned. "But you must be rewarded for such a good deed."

"It would be reward enough if you would forget the fox hunt," Akoya said softly. "There is goodness in all creatures, from the smallest of dragonflies to the largest of foxes. If you leave the foxes alone and allow me to live at the inn with my aging parents, I promise you rice will always grow green and strong in your fields."

The landowner was amused by such a simple request. "With greatest pleasure, honorable one," he said.

So it was that Akoya returned to the simple life she once knew at the roadside inn, while the fox double lived in glorious splendor at the landowner's mansion. The foxes, meanwhile, never went hungry again, and the rice flourished in the village fields forever.

In memory of Archie Langston, the original storyteller …
and for Dad, Darrell and Brendan.
L.L.

To the children of the world, may your lives be filled
with happiness.
V.B.

Text copyright © 1998 Laura Langston
Illustration copyright © 1998 Victor Bosson

Canadian Cataloguing in Publication Data
Langston, Laura, 1958–
The fox's kettle

ISBN 1-55143-130-0

I. Bosson, Victor, 1946– II. Title.
PS8573.A5832F69 1998   jC813'.54   C97-911111-0
PZ7.L27Fo 1998

Library of Congress Catalog Card Number: 97-81097

Orca Book Publishers gratefully acknowledges the support of our publishing programs provided by the following agencies: the Department of Canadian Heritage, The Canada Council for the Arts, and the British Columbia Ministry of Small Business, Tourism and Culture.

Design by Victor Bosson

Printed and bound in Hong Kong

Orca Book Publishers
PO Box 5626, Station B
Victoria, BC Canada
V8R 6S4

Orca Book Publishers
PO Box 468
Custer, WA USA
98240-0468

98 99 00   5 4 3 2 1